Dear God . . .

letters to God from a mother

Liz Hinds

First published in 1998 by
KEVIN MAYHEW LTD
Rattlesden
Bury St Edmunds
Suffolk IP30 0SZ

0 1 2 3 4 5 6 7 8 9

ISBN 1 84003 175 1
Catalogue No 1500188

Cover design by Jaquetta Sergeant
Edited by David Gatward
Typesetting by Louise Selfe
Printed and bound in Great Britain

Contents

Introduction

A short while ago, after writing an article for a women's magazine, I was asked for a mini-biography of 'about 100-150 words' to go with it. 'Yes, fine,' I said, and jotted down some details: married to Mike, mother of three children – Anna, Robert and Neil – housewife and wannabe freelance writer. When I'd finished I did a quick word count – it came to fifty-eight words. This was slightly worrying. Was that all there was to me? Could forty-five years be summed up in a sentence? Thankfully, God, being God, soon found a way to make me think again. The writings which make up this book express something of the real me, the one God alone normally sees. If you can relate to any of them, be reassured, you are not alone.

PS. At our church Writers' Group meetings we are in the habit of issuing 'disclaimers' before we read aloud any of our work. These run along the lines of, 'It's been a busy week and I only managed to scribble down some thoughts at the last moment', or, 'I couldn't get to grips with the topic so I wrote on something else', or 'The cat was sick on/the hamster ate the original and this is all I can remember of it'. Please assume all of these and many more excuses for what you are about to read.

Dear reader

Today I had a fit of the vapours. Well, almost. What actually happened was that I was in my local supermarket and I turned a corner expecting to find porridge and what I found instead was washing powder.

Why do the powers that be do it? Shopping is stressful enough without my little routine being disrupted. First they change the packaging so what was a simple matter, of recognising and selecting, becomes a time-consuming, thought-requiring act. It also results in me being marked out as the nutter to be avoided as I wander around muttering under my breath.

Then they change the layout of the store so I go home without half the things I need simply because my automatic pilot is subject to interference beyond its control.

I don't like change. Which makes what I am about to say next even more remarkable.

In the course of writing this collection, I have changed. Not simply because of writing it, although I'm sure that's been instrumental in making me aware of it. I don't like saying 'God spoke to me' but I have no doubt that through a variety of means he has been drumming a message home. Strangely, the major part has been played by a secular novel, one of a series written by Susan Howatch based around the Anglican church, although it was backed up by plenty of other things. A key phrase for one of the characters in the book was 'be the person God created you to be'.

Now the message that each of us is unique, a special individual loved by God just as we are, isn't a new one. It's one I've heard plenty of times before. It's one I've agreed to, said 'yes' to, even remembered for a while. But being the person God created me to be, wanting to be that person, or just liking that person has, for a long time, been a problem.

Dear God

There's so much I want to say, I don't know where to start.

Thank you for the events of the last few months: for the opportunity to write these letters at just the right time; for the changes in me that they reveal; for the changes themselves; for an increasing awareness of who I am; for the desire to be that person; for the releasing of the 'me-ness' that has been buried for too long; for the realisation that who I am is who you want me to be, not a poor carbon copy of someone else.

That all sounds very self-centred but, God, it's only through your doing that I am able to get to this point of security. I pray that you will use what I am for your purposes, that any writing skill I have, little though it be (not perfectly assured yet!), you will take and use. I also ask that this time it won't be a passing phase but a continually growing certainty that I am in your plan, that my role is as vital as the greatest or the least in your kingdom.

Thank you for loving me; thank you for liking me. Help me to dismiss moments of self-hatred with the confidence that comes from knowing that someone loves me completely just as I am.

I'll write again soon, but till then, lots of love,
me.

The mother's instinct

Sometimes I wonder if I've turned into a cat. If, unknowingly, I was subjected to dangerous radiation with the result that, every so often, I am transformed into a spitting, snarling, fur-flying feline. Then I look down and see that my arms are no hairier than usual, and I don't have claws instead of fingers, and I realise that the transformation is only in my mind. And the trigger? The cause of this metamorphosis? Just a mother's instinct to protect her children.

When they're babies, it's physical danger that gets this instinct flapping. As they get older, the danger becomes less obvious.

As I sit outside school waiting to collect my children, a girl of Anna's age comes out of the gate. She's attractive and slim, and I feel anger burning in me again. She was one of those who, seven years before, made Anna's life miserable at school, a bully.

And there are others, others who in some way or another have hurt my children, who seem to get away scot-free. I want to shout at the world, tell everyone what they've done. My children wouldn't thank me for it; they'd die of embarrassment. They'll never know what this pussycat is capable of.

Dear God

*I hate him. I hate him for the pain he caused. I hate him
because he's unaware of the damage he did to a fragile heart.
I hate him for not loving her. I'm glad he doesn't love her!
I don't want him near her! I don't want a repetition of this
anguish. How dare he not love her? How could he not love her?*

*I shouldn't talk of hate in a letter to you. But you hated too.
You hated those who hurt your children. You understand, don't
you?*

*I thought that I'd been through all this teenage angst for
myself and that was that. I didn't know you had to go through
it again for your children. No, not for, but with. I wish it was
for. I wish I could take the pain for them. They're too precious
to suffer. Is this how you feel when you see us hurt? How do
you bear it? How can you not interfere? But you don't, you let
us learn, you wait and hold and caress, until we can turn from
our misery to you.*

But why does it have to hurt so much?

Love, me.

When I grow up

'I want to be a professional skateboarder.'

'A fish slice fighter.' (You had to be there.)

'A writer I suppose.'

Pathetic! Not a lawyer or stockbroker between them. Who's going to keep us in our old age in the manner to which we'd like to become accustomed, that's what I want to know? Where's their driving ambition? Aren't they interested in being successful, or making money?

Ah, just remembered we're Christians, we know that success isn't measured by the type of car you drive or which part of town you live in, or even how much you tithe. No, a truly successful person is one who is living his life for God, who finds fulfilment in being all that God intended him to be. If that means struggling on the bread-line while serving God, then praise the Lord, brother! So there should be no pressure to do well, pass exams, get into college, find a job, be successful. Bleep! Bleep! Warning! Parent Alarm! Parent Alarm!

I want my children to do well, pass exams, get into college, find a job, be successful.

Oh, oh, guilt is creeping in here; what sort of Christian mother are you to be so concerned with the human aspects of life? Don't you believe there are more important things than money or success?

I've been struggling with this but I think the answer lies in something I've just noticed I wrote above (a speedy answer to prayer, that!) – '. . . all that God intended him to be'. God gives each of us different gifts, but if we put them in the back of the cupboard along with Auntie Doreen's bath salts, then we're being ungrateful, not to say wasteful. On the other hand, if we use those gifts, we show our gratitude. God's equipped us to be the people he wants us to be, and he expects us to take full advantage, but things don't just happen, we have to do our bit. And if that means staying in at nights swotting to make sure you do your best in exams, well, praise the Lord, sister!

Dear God

Is it wrong to want the best for your children? To want them to get on and succeed? I don't think so; it's what you want for us isn't it? Thankfully though, you don't pile on the pressure quite so much. I don't mean to, I don't want to nag. It's just that sometimes I think they're capable of doing better than they do and I get annoyed because they've let themselves down, particularly if it's for a bad reason.

They're very capable academically, they could do well. Help them to take advantage of the gifts you've given them, to use every bit of their talent and skill in whatever field; don't let it be wasted, Lord. Help them to be the people you intend them to be, to live life to the full, all the time knowing they're following your path for them. It's great that you have plans for us, for our benefit. Let them feel the excitement of waiting for what's in store, but help them also see clearly what they have to do to bring your plans to fruition.

Help me to stand back; to support, not nag; to encourage, not dishearten; to be thankful, not moan; to have reasonable expectations, not mountain-high hopes. Don't let me compare them with others and be proud or envious. Don't let me try and force them into the shape I think they should be, but let me enjoy watching them grow into the individuals you want them to be.

Love, me.

PS Lord, do you get fed up with these requests to do this, let me be that, help me here, etc? Sorry, there seem to be a lot in this letter. Will try and do better!

14

The future's bright

It's January as I write this and, all being well, next autumn Anna will set off for university, a normal and natural happening and one that thousands of families experience every year. So why am I dreading it so much?

Perhaps dread is the wrong word. Of course I'm pleased with her progress and success, and preparing the children for independent living is part of parenting, I know all that. It still doesn't stop me feeling bereft at just the thought of home without her, even temporarily.

My depression reached its climax over Christmas (you should have been here, I was a bundle of fun to be around). It's amazing how one thought can lead to another: I started off thinking, 'This is our last proper Christmas before things start changing. First it'll be Anna off, after that the boys in turn, and before we know where we are, it'll be just the two of us, and they'll probably go and work at different ends of the country and we'll hardly ever see them, and really when you think about it, what is the purpose of life anyway?' As I said, a bundle of joy.

The thing with negativity, I find, is that it's hard to get out of, and it was in this self-centred depressed mood that I went along to the weekly prayer meeting. I said my amens in the right place but my heart wasn't in it. Most of the time I sat there thinking, 'If God's so good why doesn't he tell someone how I'm feeling so they can pray for me?' At the same time I battled with pride. I wasn't going to share how I felt – what, tell someone what an idiot I was – you must be joking!

But desperation won in the end. After the meeting I spoke to someone I knew and respected even though we weren't particularly close, and, afterwards, we sat in the dark in the car and chatted and prayed. It wasn't an instant cure but within a couple of days, I gradually became aware that the weight in my stomach was lifting, and that there did seem to be a purpose to life again. Now there's a coincidence!

15

In many ways it was the chat that helped. It made me remember that even if her family concerns weren't exactly the same as mine at that moment, Lucy, like mothers everywhere, had worries about her children, and sharing hers helped me to go away with a clearer mind. (I'm sure that sounds illogical the way it's written but I hope you get my drift – 'a trouble shared', etc.)

It didn't end there either. The following Sunday Lucy checked up on me, and said that God had reminded her to pray for me on occasions during the week. Isn't God great? And isn't it brilliant being part of his caring family?

But don't stand too close to me next September, or you may get washed away on a sea of tears!

Dear God

Oh, Lord, what do you think when you see your children in the slimy pit getting more and more bogged down? Do you wish we'd just look up and see the hand held out ready to grab us if only we'd reach out?

I'm sorry (again) that I seem to look down and in more than up and out. Don't you ever feel like saying, 'Tough cookies, you got in there, you can get yourself out!'? It's horrid being in despair, especially when you know it's of your own making, and irrational.

I am grateful, Lord. Grateful that my children are progressing well through their lives, that they're developing the skills necessary to become independent. I'm thankful for their academic abilities and glad that Anna is making plans for university. I know in my heart this is what it's all about, preparing them and letting them go, but, Lord, it doesn't half hurt. And that's just the thought of it, we're not even there yet. What am I going to be like when Anna sets off for the first time?

Because children leaving home, for whatever reason, is such a normal thing to happen, I've never thought about how the parents feel, what emotions run through them. I've never realised the wrench, the change – perhaps that's it, Lord. Perhaps I need to look at this, not as a tragedy, but as a change, a right and proper change, indeed one that is a mark of parental success: 'You've done a good job, I'm glad I loaned this child to you, trusted you with the awesome responsibility of preparing her for adulthood. I have great plans for her, your child, my child.'

Help me to let go, Lord, not to hang on screaming, not to inflict guilt or distaste. Help me to look forward to a relationship that matures and develops and grows in love and trust.

It's going to be so hard, Lord, please help me.

Love, me.

Do you work?

It's such a simple question, but I'm always getting caught out. I suppose I could argue that the questioner is at fault, that he, or maybe she, should be more specific.

If I was asked, 'Do you have paid employment?', it would be no problem. As it is, the question is invariably, 'Do you work?' and before I know where I am my mouth has gone into overdrive, accompanied by a suitable 'I'm unworthy' shoulder shrug.

'No, I don't.'

At that, I'm either dismissed as a woolly-headed housewife or I'm treated to a look of amazement and asked, 'Well, wouldn't you like a nice little part-time job?'

No, I don't want a flippin' part-time job! I have enough trouble getting my life into any sort of order as it is. Anyway, all I've ever wanted to be is a wife and mother. I gave up the idea of being a vet when I saw a television programme about one and he had his hand stuck up a cow's bottom.

The trouble is that, nowadays, the majority of women do go back to 'work' at some stage of their children's lives, and it's getting earlier and earlier. As I said, I have no great desire to find paid employment, but as usual my ever-ready guilt complex creeps up and accuses me of laziness and I know there's some truth in that as well, hence my confusion.

Dear God

Who am I? While other people lie awake at night wondering if there is a God, I lie awake wondering if there is a me. I wasn't always like this, this uncertainty has crept up on me over the last few years.

I used to know who I was. I was someone's wife, someone's mother. Now the children are getting older and my role is less clearly defined. Society's view is that I should be going out to work at least part-time, to earn some money, contribute to the family. I don't like a society which judges us by how much we earn or what we've achieved (and I know that's not how you view us), but I still feel guilty because I'm not doing anything 'worthwhile'. I cook (sometimes), clean (even less). I do buy food and wash clothes. I've started writing but I could no more say, in reply to the question, 'what do you do?' that I'm a writer than I could claim to be a brain surgeon. I enjoy writing but I don't make much money from it, therefore it is a waste of time. And what right really have I to expect to be kept at home?

The trouble is whatever I do, I feel I should be doing something else. I'm disorganised and my life seems to be in constant turmoil between what I want to do and what I think I should be doing. I rather suspect that I'm a waste of space.

I have the kind of life many women would give their eye teeth for, so why am I so confused? Answers on a postcard please, God, because I'm not awfully good at listening.

Love, maybe me.

Eyes up!

This is a crucial year for our family. Come June, Anna will be taking her A-levels and Robert his GCSEs. Passers-by would be well-advised to give our house a wide berth to avoid being caught in a maelstrom of anxiety, depression, fatigue and short temper, and that's just me.

When the pressure's on it's difficult to avoid getting bogged down, to see anything but the need to pass exams, to get on. The temptation is to nag, only from the best motives of course! But how many of us respond well to this kind of persuasion?

I suppose the ideal is to encourage gently and be supportive, but that's easier said than done when it's midnight and you're about to check an assignment that has to be in the following day. Surely even the wonderful Jane Asher would be hard-pressed to smile beatifically at that point!

The way I react to my children all depends on the sort of day I've had. If it's gone well, I can make friendly enquiries about their day and not blow my top if they've failed to hand in work on time or forgotten to prepare for the maths test. On the other hand, if I'm regretting having got up that morning, then heaven help them if they've failed to hand in work!

That's not fair on them; they should be able to expect consistency from me, but that's the way it is. Maybe it's good for them to appreciate that grown-ups, even mums and dads, have bad days. I could spend a lot of time condemning myself for not being perfect. It's good to have an ideal and to strive to attain it, but I have to be realistic and accept the fact that quite often I will fail, and when that happens I might have to apologise to my children. Then again sometimes they deserve to be shouted at!

So this coming year, when all I can see is revision, grumbling, boredom and the torture of exams, I hope I remember a lesson I've learnt walking the cliffs: if you're afraid to lift your eyes from the ground in case you walk in dog poo, you're going to miss an awful lot of pleasure.

Dear God

As we approach this next season, help us to remember that that is what it is: a season which will be over in a comparatively short time.

Help us not to nag but to be encouraging, to draw out the best from the children, to expect the best they are capable of, and not to put them down. Give us patience and the peace that comes from knowing you are in control and that all things work for good for your children.

Help them to prepare thoroughly, not to over-tire themselves but to apply themselves realistically. To be aware of what is necessary, to want to do their best, to not let themselves down. Help us not to be so engrossed in exam preparation that we forget that there is life outside textbooks.

And whatever happens, whether the results are what they hoped for, or a disappointment, help us all to keep it in proportion.

And please keep them healthy for this important year.

Love, me.

Eat for your life

It wouldn't be too far from the mark to say that, as a family, we've all got healthy appetites. My weekly grocery bill proves that beyond all reasonable doubt! I suppose I first suspected it years ago when I went to collect my son from a friend's house. He'd been there for tea and, when I arrived, was just wiping his plate clean. The mother of the house looked at him and said, 'He eats well, doesn't he?' Maybe I was being ultra-sensitive but I took that to mean he'd eaten them out of house and home. Well, you don't normally comment on how well a child eats, do you?

Now this will sound insensitive and definitely not politically correct, but bearing in mind what I've said about my family, if one of them leaves as much as a slice of carrot, we tend to make a joke of it and say, 'What's the matter? Are you anorexic or something?'

After all that, you'd think that if one member of the family started not being hungry at mealtimes, I'd have noticed. But I didn't. No, I did notice. I noticed Anna losing weight, I even suspected that she was being sick, but when she denied it so coolly, I believed her and put it down to, well, I don't know what. I just thought it couldn't happen to her I suppose.

It wasn't until months later, after the crisis had passed, that she told me what she'd been through, how she'd felt about a boy who'd let her down and how it had caused her to lose interest in life.

Dear God

What went wrong? How could I be so unaware of the pain my daughter was going through? Why did she feel she could only talk to others and not me? Yet, Lord, I am so glad (yet again) of your presence with her, even in her darkest moments when she didn't want to know you, I know you were there, reaching out, waiting.

What would I do without you? Knowing you never leave them alone is such reassurance. Whether it's in a crowded nightclub or tear-wetted bed, you're there and closer to them than I can ever be. That means so much, Lord. I can't begin to express how grateful I am to you, and how much I depend on you.

But, Father, what happened? What went wrong? She's beautiful, intelligent, gentle and caring. How could she lose her interest in life and care so little for everything.

Lord, I'm so thankful that you were around, that you rescued her before her eating problem took hold. It was all down to you, Lord, and I thank you from the bottom of my heart.

Heaps of love, me.

What does she look like?

Anna is nearly eighteen. She will soon come of age, be able to vote, have all the privileges associated with being an adult – she will have the right to have her lip pierced.

Then again, she says, she might have a tattoo.

There are times I despair of my daughter. She grumbles that people stare at her in the street, and she looks comparatively normal now.

Maybe she's only making threats, flaunting her rights. Maybe she doesn't intend to go ahead with it, it's just a way of teasing her poor old folks. Maybe I'll be voted Miss Baywatch 1998.

Just the thought of having a needle stuck through my lip is enough for me to need a long lie-down. If I try to imagine what it's like to have a perpetual ulcer and an irritating ring hanging about my mouth, urgh, urgh!

It started when she was about fourteen. She had her ears pierced; I had mine done at the same time. Then it was a ring at the top of her ear; I didn't bother. Much later it was her belly button; I gave up.

I don't understand this obsession she has, but my prayers are simple.

Dear God

*Keep her safe. I'm glad that she has had the sense to go to
clean, reputable establishments. The danger of infection is
my greatest worry. What I think it looks like doesn't matter,
all that matters is that she's safe, so please continue to
protect her.*

*I would rather she had neither a tattoo nor her lip pierced,
but whatever she does I'll still love her. But please, if there's
any chance, I would appreciate it if you could use your influence
to talk her out of it.*

I leave her and this decision in your hands.

Love, me.

Hair today, gone tomorrow

Well, it finally happened. You can't say we didn't warn her. We tried our best to be good parents and made sure she understood the risks she was taking, but would she listen? No. So it's her own fault. On her own head be it. Or not, as the case may be.

It all started with the gold pipe cleaners. No, thinking about it, it started long ago, when Anna decided that hair wasn't something you just washed and brushed, but a fashion accessory, which could change colour to suit her outfit for the night. Our cries of, 'It'll all fall out if you keep doing that', were pooh-poohed, and she kept doing it. From blue to red to purple to all the colours of the rainbow. She was undeterred by the fact that old ladies avoided her and little children pointed at her in the street. Cutting her hair short, rather than depriving her of variety of style, offered a whole new dimension which is where the pipe cleaners come in. She used them to create a crowd of mini-bunches which stuck out at right-angles from her scalp. Unfortunately this exaggerated the redness of her hair – a totally out-of-a-bottle red, of course. So the teachers complained. She then decided that she'd bleach it, her logic being that, after all, blonde is a natural colour so they couldn't complain, could they? Well, that would have been all right if her hair hadn't gone pink and started to fall out. Which is the point at which we said, 'Told you so'.

In spite of frantic telephone calls to school the next day, it was still tellings-off and tears and a rush to buy yet more dye to turn it brown this time. 'You've got to help me, you've got to sort this out!' (I forgot to mention that we'd hacked off all the pink bits so her hair is really short now.)

So by the end of the second day we had just about achieved a suitably boring look, which wouldn't get her into trouble, and what do I find her doing? Putting red hair mousse on to liven it up! At that point I left the room screaming.

There's a bit in the gospels where Jesus says you don't have to pray long complicated prayers, and that kept me going all through the night as each time I woke up, worried and prayed this.

Lord

Please don't let her wake up
  to find all her hair on the pillow.
Don't let it fall out,
    pleeease . . .

Retrospective

'I don't ever want to grow up.'

There are times I wish that, like Peter Pan, I could have stayed a child for ever, but it wasn't to be. The day I grew up was the day the protective lying had to stop, the day no one would say, 'Don't worry, it'll be all right.' Welcome to the world of sorrow and pain and death; in other words, welcome to reality.

Anna grew up last year. Her life which until then had been a success story suddenly turned sour and she experienced failure, rejection and all the emotional turmoil that accompanies those visitors. And there was nothing I could do about it. I was barely aware of it.

Dear God

It is so hard to stand by and see my children suffer for whatever reason. The desire to do something to change the situation is overwhelming but in actual fact there is nothing I can do. They're growing up, I know, and part of growing up is learning to deal with real life. I'm so glad, yet again, that you are in their lives, that you are the best one to help them through this maze. Keep your hand firmly around them, God, and guide and guard them. Thank you that, for each of us, you are there in our blackest moments, even if it doesn't feel like it, and that you hang on in there, carrying us and waiting for the moment we realise and turn again to you.

Help me to be a similar invisible presence, there when I'm needed but knowing when to stand back and let them get on with it even if it means biting my tongue. Help me to be supportive but not over-protective. Let me trust you for them as you trust me with them.

Love, me.

Not a question of trust

Robert is an expert at avoiding the question. I have learnt to choose my phrases carefully. 'Have you moved the Sellotape?' will elicit a negative reply, even though he might know where the Sellotape is, and he knows that I'm only asking because I want to use it. It would be far too helpful and simple to volunteer, 'It's on the kitchen shelf', for example. So we have to go through a range of questions like 'Have you seen/moved/touched?' in order to determine the answer. (To ask, 'Do you know where it is?' is just as pointless as he replies, 'Yes/no'.)

Depending on my/his mood, we can survive this regular Question Time, though I do feel like Sir Robin Day on occasions. But sometimes it just doesn't work.

Take the other evening for example (preferably as far away as possible). Anna's pen had gone missing and she was accusing her darling brother of having something to do with it. They came into the kitchen and I started my usual practice of working through the questions. Through all this Robert was chuckling and refusing to look up. I stood up for him in the face of Anna's accusations, stating that he would not lie to me. And my reward for this? He turns round and accuses me of not believing him and calling him a liar. A short screaming match ensued with me giving up and him flouncing out. I ended up apologising, trying to explain. Should I have done that? I don't know.

Oh, and incidentally, it turned out that it was me who had thrown Anna's pen away, so she was mad at me too.

Dear God

So it's not just girls. Not just girls who have moods, are irritable and touchy, and totally unreasonable.

I wish, Lord, I had just a fraction of your wisdom and judgement, and a whole load of tact and patience. I know that, basically, Robert is very kind and generous and loving, and I do appreciate his sense of humour, but I wish that he could see things from my point of view sometimes. I want to believe him and I do really, he just makes it hard for me to be convinced. Of course, if I just say, 'Robert's not lying, he is innocent of whatever misdemeanour you are accusing him', I know what will happen. Either the right question won't have been asked, or I'll be accused of favouritism and 'It's not fair'.

It's not fair, Lord. I'm in a no-win situation here and I'm inclined to give up, to step back and not get involved. To say, 'Sort it out for yourselves', but that doesn't work either. Being able to trust each other and to know that we are trusted in return is so important.

Please help me to take time to stop, listen, think, question, and generally play peacemaker. Please give me the wisdom, patience and sense of humour to deal fairly in disputes.

Love, me.

It's not fair

'Mum, he hit me.'

'Oi!, you hit me first.'

'Only because you wouldn't let me pass.'

'You didn't ask, did you?'

'I did too.'

'WILL YOU BOTH SHUT UP!'

Nobody prepared me for this. An only child, I grew up on the Famous Five and *Little Women*, children all mucking in together and helping each other. Yes, storybook children fell out but it was soon sorted. It's not like that in real life. In real life I alternate, depending on my mood, between trying to get to the root of the trouble, and giving up and screaming at everybody. Sometimes I even resort to the third alternative – telling them to clear off and fight it out for themselves. (That usually follows an emotional little speech, delivered in a weak and quivery voice, about how I've tried my best, I can't do any more, and if that's all they think of me, they can . . . it usually does the guilt trick but you can't play it too often.)

It really upsets me, though, that they seem to dislike each other so much. My dreams of a close-knit family sharing the good and bad times disappeared into thin air a while ago. Maybe it's because I was an only child that I find it so hard; others assure me that it's quite normal for siblings to fight. I suppose they do have times when they enjoy each other's company and maybe those times will increase as they get older, but, at the moment, they're so few and far between, the in-between bits weigh more heavily.

Maybe they need a common enemy to fight, a smuggler or a pirate, but harmless baddies are a bit thin on the ground around here. Come back, Enid Blyton, all is forgiven.

Dear God

Is it meant to be like this? Is it normal? I am so fed up with the squabbles and the fights and trying to act as judge in these situations. Have we done something wrong in the way that we've brought them up? They don't see us fight and bicker. We always try to be fair and not have favourites yet they always insist that they, whichever one it is, are the most hard done by.

'It's not fair, he started it!'

'You're always picking on me.'

The temptation to yell at and punish them all seems unfair on the innocent. But is there ever a truly innocent party? I don't know; I wasn't there when it started. If I question them the cause goes back further and further until it's impossible to decide; I don't think they are lying or deliberately trying to mislead me. It's just that they can always find an excuse for their actions — not even an excuse as far as they're concerned, it's the truth. Each little punch can be traced back to an earlier niggle, and another little injustice is chalked up against me. It's not fair, Lord, whatever I do, I always end up as the guilty one.

You have the advantage, Lord, being omnipresent and omniscient. You know whose fault it is; you're not misled by me putting the blame on someone else. It would be easier for me if you were. But really I'm glad, it means I don't have to pretend or lie, I know I can't fool you. You've seen me at my worst and you still love me. You don't compare me unfavourably with others.

Would I love my children whatever they did? Of course. I think they know that. I hope they do. Help me treat each of them as an individual, not to compare them with each other or others. And help me to do the same with myself.

Love, me.

'You've got to kiss
a lot of frogs . . .'

Once upon a time there was a lovely princess. She had everything she wanted . . . except her handsome prince. Her fairy godmother came along and said, 'Don't be sad. Here is a prince for you.' And just like magic, he appeared. The princess was happy for a while but then she realised that the prince was not a prince at all but a frog – a very kind and gentle frog, but a frog nonetheless. She said to him, 'Goodbye. I am sorry, it's not your fault.' She said to her fairy godmother, 'Thank you for trying.' And the princess went back to her tower and continued to dream of the prince who didn't love her.

Sometimes it can seem like a fairy story the way things happen just at the right time. Like the time Anna was pining over her lost love, and who should appear but a lovely Christian boy who asked her out and was keen to see more of her. I was delighted and thanked God for this timely appearance. Here was someone who would take her mind off the other one, help rebuild her confidence and look after her. Wow, great!

So what does she do? She finished with him because 'it's not fair on him because I keep comparing them and it's unfavourable'.

'Well, couldn't you try for a bit longer, you might grow to . . . ?'

'No, I've kissed my prince, everyone else will always be a frog.'

Dear God

Well, you tried. It seemed a brilliant idea to me, sending along the answer to a mother's prayer like that. I'm sorry she didn't take you up on it. He seemed a nice boy. It would have been so simple. I should have known life wouldn't be that simple.

I suppose she needs time and space. She's so convinced that he was the right one for her. Why can't she see all the bad things about him? Why does she only remember the good? Why can't I say something helpful?

I suppose that even if it only lasted a short time, the new relationship helped by helping her to sort out her thoughts, by making her feel wanted and desirable. Maybe that was all you intended, maybe it was me who was set on making a big thing of it. Maybe you know she has to do it a bit at a time, to realise that there are lots of princes out there, one of whom is the one you have in mind for her. The one who will truly be the right one.

As always, you know best. We just muddle along, but, gosh, life isn't half complicated.

Love, me.

Why doesn't he phone?

Boys are scum bags. Unreliable, untrustworthy good-for-nothings who wouldn't recognise true worth if it jumped up and bit them. Well, OK, not all boys maybe. My sons aren't like that, and neither are yours, I'm sure. Maybe it's just the boys that Anna gets involved with. She seems to have an uncanny knack of picking them. Even the Christian ones, whom you might expect to be different, turn out just as unreliable. I feel quite murderous towards them. Apparently genetic scientists are working on a way of improving the sense of smell. They've been successful with mice and rats, and are looking to improve the drug-sniffing abilities of dogs. Now if the scientists wanted to do something really useful, they could train dogs to genetically sniff out undesirable boyfriends. Maybe Anna would take advice from Harvey, our dog. She certainly won't take it from me. Any comment from me along the lines of 'He looks like a nice boy' guarantees a scrunching up of face and an emphatic 'Urghhh, no!' Unless a boy is into dyed hair, body piercing and/or tattoos, she doesn't seem interested. Not that I think that any of those things necessarily make for untrustworthiness, it just seems to be working out that way.

Dear God,

I'm torn here. Anna is in her final A-level year and doesn't really have the time to get involved with a boy. On the other hand, all her friends have found boys and seem to be balancing things OK at the moment, and I don't want her to feel left out or a loner or undesirable. Then again, suppose she did find a boyfriend and suppose he broke her heart just before the exams. Pouf, that's it – exams, university plans, future career, potentially all up the spout. (You know I always look on the bright side, Lord!)

Lord, you and I know just how special she is. How loving and kind and gentle. How she constantly encourages her friends, never knocks them. The heart she has for the homeless. Her talents and abilities. And we know, you even more than me, how she's been battered this last year, how her confidence and self-esteem have been worn down. I'm so glad that you've been with her in her darkest moments, and I ask you, knowing your answer already, to keep on carrying and supporting and loving her.

Help her to believe that her worth doesn't depend on the boyfriend on her arm, and to know that when the time is right, you will ensure she meets the right boy, the one for her who will see what we see and will value her above all others.

But waiting, boyfriendless, is hard, so please help her to be patient and not sad.

Love, me.

Sex before marriage

There's one thing parents and children are agreed on: the thought of the other 'doing it' is too appalling to be contemplated. Children prefer the idea of immaculate conception to the thought of their parents involved in any night-time activity; and parents earnestly hope that their children will remain uncorrupted and uninterested until the matrimonial bed, at the very earliest.

In reality both know their hopes have a shaky foundation. 'I know you do it; I just don't want to think about it,' daughter comments. And I wonder how long it will be before I'm saying the same about her.

At the moment we're safe, relationships haven't lasted long enough to become dangerous (I'm sure she's sensible enough to say 'no' to casual sex) but that's not necessarily the case for her friends. Their behaviour has caused her to question me, and God, about it. She's not happy with what seems to be the answer, and I'm struggling to find good reasons myself.

Dear God

I'd like a clear answer to this one, Lord, none of my favourite, 'Because I say so'. It's a question I'm going to have to answer soon; in fact, it's already been raised and I've stumbled over the answer. So, should sex only ever be within marriage? What if two people are in a long-term stable relationship, they love each other and want to express their love physically, is it wrong then?

I suppose experts would say that you intended sex to be part of marriage and virginity to be something you give to the person you want to spend the rest of your life with. But why? To avoid unnecessary pain? If a long-term relationship breaks up, the pain is terrible. I don't think it's any less painful if the couple aren't sleeping together. I'm not talking about casual, one night affairs, which of course are wrong, for all sorts of reasons. That's not the problem.

What if any one of my children, sometime in the future, knowing what the church teaches, comes to make their own decision, and chooses sex outside marriage? Will you condemn them? Should I? I can't.

Please answer me soon and with good reasons, reasons I can put forward which aren't just because I say so. I'm sorry if this sounds stroppy but my stroppiness isn't directed at you, rather at me, because I take so many things for granted without really thinking why.

Love, me.

Natural birth control

There's one form of birth control even the Pope couldn't object to, seeing as it was God's idea. Well, what other reason did he have for creating children?

The only surprise is that the world isn't made up of one-child families. The exhaustion that accompanies each little bundle of joy turns out to be a highly effective weapon in the sibling battle-field. A sort of pre-emptive strike. 'If I wear out my mum and dad, and make sure I cry at appropriate intervals throughout the night, I'll never have to share them with anyone.'

Strangely, most parents have bad memories. How else can you explain the fact that no sooner does the infant start to sleep more and life becomes easier than it suddenly seems a good idea to have another one? Or perhaps it's been so long since the parents have had the opportunity, they've forgotten what the end result could be.

Anyway the years pass and before you know where you are, you've got teenagers in the house. Teenagers who stay up later than you, and who, you suspect, hear and analyse every sound emanating from your room.

By the time they leave home you have neither the inclination nor the energy to celebrate – you've probably forgotten how to do it anyway.

Dear God

I love my children dearly, you know that. But do they have to stay awake so late, or rush into our room first thing in the morning? And would it be too much to ask that they all sleep out on the same night, just occasionally?

Trendy preachers are fond of telling us that sex is God's creation and meant to be enjoyed, they don't say when or how. It is a wonderful gift that you gave us, and I am really grateful for it and for a loving husband who's still interested in a slightly podgy, slightly greying me. But it's not just a question of finding the right time and place.

Lord, I'm so tired when I go to bed, my mind is reeling with the events of the day, and I need to relax. Making love needs a certain amount of physical and emotional energy which isn't always there – reading is so much easier. But then I feel that I'm letting him down, making him feel unwanted, maybe even unloved, and sometimes we seem to drift apart.

Please help us to appreciate each other in all that we do, to find alternative ways of showing love, to have the energy to enjoy each other, to make the opportunities, and to remember how to!

Love, me.

The lost children

Have you noticed how the news seems to be getting sillier these days? The number of times I've heard a report then looked at the calendar convinced it must be April 1st. If it's not cows falling out of the sky, then it's cloned sheep, or even humans. Summer used to be regarded as the 'silly season' for news but it happens all year round now. And what could be sillier than an art exhibition which features a tent covered in the names of those with whom the artist has slept? Or sillier than the same artist claiming that it was an abortion which released her gift, her true creativity. At least it would be silly if it wasn't so appalling.

Dear God

I don't know what to say, except I'm sorry. I don't know how we've got in this state, where sex is taken apart from love and procreation and treated as a commodity, an experience whose side-effects can be disregarded, discarded. I can't start to imagine the effect on the lives of the women who have undergone abortions. More and more women are speaking out now, some unfortunately saying, 'So what? It's nothing, no problem!' Can they really mean that? Will their words come back and haunt them when they least expect it? I hope not, for their sakes.

Lord, I know there are many women who have felt forced into abortion for all sorts of reasons; some who do it, not unwillingly exactly, but as a last resort because they're at the end of their tether, and who will mourn for their lost children. But for each of those there are some who use abortion as a sort of contraceptive device or who care too much for other things to be bothered to have their babies. Lord, what kind of society are we?

But, God, having said all that, having decried motives, I can't totally oppose the act of abortion. I feel guilty when I read of pro-life campaigns and hear about Christians marching and speaking out, when I'm so woolly as usual. It's like euthanasia, I can't condemn that completely. I just don't know.

If I had your wisdom, knowledge, and most of all, love, maybe I could feel more sure about what's right and what's wrong. I would know. In each situation I could judge, but as it is, I don't have one fraction of your insight, and I can't be so positive.

Then again, I do have your Spirit in me, and if you will guide me I will understand more. But surely, even then, it's individuals you care about, not rules. 'Thou shalt not have an abortion under any circumstance' isn't one of your commandments. But 'Thou shalt not kill' is.

I don't know, I'm so confused. You hate the sin but love the sinner. You show compassion and forgiveness. You bring healing to broken lives, broken hearts, broken bodies. It's up to you to forgive and us to support. It's up to us to speak out against sin but also to try to understand.

I would not want my child to have an abortion but if she did, there is no way I would condemn and abandon her. She would need my support more than ever. But I would weep for her and her lost child. And at the other end of our lives, who can really know what they would do in desperate situations? Maybe some can say definitely, but not me.

God, give me wisdom, understanding and compassion. Help me to speak up to condemn wrongdoing and abortion for convenience's sake. Put into high places those who can speak out clearly, and always let them retain your compassion. Give back to this nation its concern for unborn children, Lord. And give us the compassion to love and support those who have had abortions, and at last learn to love rather than condemn.

Love, me.

Over the limit

It's very important when you're young to conform, to fit in, to be like the rest. Now in most respects I'm about as conformist and boring as you can imagine, so to find that, in one way at least, I was different came as a surprise. Now don't panic, I don't have six toes or anything like that (well, I do actually but that's another story). No, my little foible is much more mundane, and these days, less unusual than it was twenty years ago – I don't drink. Alcohol that is. Not for any high-minded principle I hasten to add. I just don't like the taste. So my view of life has always been rather sober; I've never seen it through an alcoholic haze. Perhaps if I had, if I'd experienced inside looking out, I wouldn't find drunkenness so disgusting.

It's not the helpless alcoholics on the streets that upset me, at least not in the same way. It's the effects of social drinking amongst the so-called respectable classes I struggle with. A seventeen year old who can't stand up and quietly slides down a wall. A seventy year old who can't walk in a straight line and stumbles and falls; just mild cases.

Drunkenness is degrading to the person involved yet it's treated as a joke by all and sundry. Tales of being out cold or drunk as a skunk are relayed . . . with pride?

Take it on a step from the family gathering, and visit the night-clubs or pubs heaving with teens, twenties, under-agers. Now we're talking real danger. If you leave simply embarrassed, you're getting off lightly. Perhaps I'm exaggerating. Perhaps I've become a prig.

My children show no signs of following me down the alcohol-free path. In fact, in spite of tales of their father as a teenager being left singing in gutters, Anna at least seems intent on learning her own lessons . . .

Dear God

It really frightens me the way alcohol is treated so casually when the effects can be so devastating. I can't see the attraction. But if you like alcohol and feel that it gives you the confidence you need, then the attraction becomes understandable, and the drinks harder to refuse. I'm thankful the lessons Anna's undergone so far have been embarrassing rather than dangerous. Keep it that way, Lord. (Actually, Lord, I hope she's learnt her lessons, if only for my sake.)

But what of the boys, Lord, when it's their turn? When the expectation is that it's normal to drink, to get drunk – will the pressures on them as macho males to conform be even greater? I don't want them to be teetotal, Lord, not unless they choose. But I do want them to be sensible, to stay in control. How easy is that, Lord? Let them see clearly the dangers. Help them to make rational, thought-out decisions they can stick with, that they'll want to stand by. Most of all, let them experience the exhilarating heights of your love, which shows up man-made highs for the falsehood they are.

But don't let me condemn, Lord. Let them feel secure to come home whatever state they're in, knowing we'll be there to pick up the pieces or clear up the mess.

Love, me.

On different sides of the path

Yesterday, I read this description of church from a children's book: 'Belonging to church means spending time with friends who believe the same things about Jesus as you do, friends who share their possessions, friends who care for each other and enjoy being together. Jesus said that the way his followers could be recognised was by the way that they loved one another.'

It sounds so simple, doesn't it? Well, it was a children's book. But doesn't it actually say something a bit like that in the Bible?

Oh yes, I suppose it does. After all, what could followers of Jesus possibly disagree about?

Are you serious? Where would you like me to start?

My local church is in crisis; it's on the verge of splitting. The rift is causing serious damage not only to the church as a whole but to the people belonging to it. It's no joke.

Dear God

This morning I came very close to quarrelling with a good friend. Me who never quarrels with anyone! We made a joke of it, and walked on different sides of the path, and talked of other things, but the wedge is in place now. Will it dig in deeper and push us further apart until we really are walking in opposite directions on different sides of the path?

It's ironic that the cause of our disagreement should be our local church. Why is our church on the verge of collapse, God? How have we gone so far from the ideal?

Lord, over the last year or so, young lives have been damaged, maybe terminally, because people like me wouldn't stand up and be counted.

'It's nothing to do with me.'

'I'm not important. What does it matter what I think?'

I cared too much for a quiet life and people's good opinion of me. But the problems didn't go away and now our church itself is dying. There are a lot of angry and hurt people, and nobody can sit on the sidelines any more. Whose side are you on, God? You must be on mine because mine is the right side.

My friend's on the other side. She wasn't at first, she was angry too, but . . . what happened? Did she listen to, and believe, half-truths? How can two people be in a meeting, listen to the same speakers and come away having heard completely different things?

Lord, help us to stay friends. Have your will in the church. I don't know what that is; I don't know how we got here; I don't know what the answer is. Except it's going to mean lots of pain.

Help.

Love, me.

Victory outreach

Our church was in turmoil. The congregation had split into factions, complete with backstabbing, 'all done in love' of course. Heads, and spirits, were drooping. Anger was rife. Our thoughts centred on whose side we were on. God seemed a long way away.

It turned out that he wasn't.

One Sunday morning a team from Victory Outreach, an organisation working with ex-convicts, drug addicts and homeless men and women, led the meeting. One by one, they gave their testimonies or sang, and the life-changing power of God, and only God, shone through.

Our church was still in a mess but God could change that too.

Dear God

You're amazing, you know that? You have this great way of lifting us out of ourselves. When we're intent on studying the ground and seeing only the obstacles on our path, you force us to look up and see what's happening in the rest of the world, or at least in the next valley.

You show us things we don't want to see; things we'd rather ignore. You show us how you don't ignore them but you do something.

And that's what you're about. Not petty squabbles and disagreements but real life getting in and getting your hands dirty; changing lives, putting together not tearing apart.

Restore clear vision to us, Lord. Remind us who the enemy really is.

Thank you, Lord.

Thank you so much.

Love, me.

Is there a god?

Come close, I'm going to whisper something. That's right, bring your head in tight. Now I'll tell you – I sometimes wonder if there is a God. Like when I'm looking at the sky and it's a clear night and there are millions of stars and I'm overwhelmed by the enormity of it all and think, 'Can there really be someone who holds all this in his hands?'

At times like that I have to bring God down to size. I don't mean that disrespectfully, I just need to be able to get my head around things. So I think of Jesus, Jesus the man; the walking, talking human being, who experienced life as we know it. Having focused on him, it's easier to accept the totally outrageous concept of an omnipotent, omnipresent, omniscient being.

If that's not enough, you don't have to look far around you for evidence of a creator. There's a large area of wasteland near our home and if you were to study just one square metre, you'd find at least ten different varieties of grass. That's not different types of flowers or plants but just grass. I mean, what's the point? It's just a piece of waste ground, no one notices what goes on there, it's not on show, up for a prize. If man had been in charge of designing it, it would have been a case of which grass provides the best 'product to effort ratio' (and no, I don't know what that means, either!)

The natural world is infinitely different. Out on the cliff path, looking at the rock formations, realising everything that must have taken place over a huge number of years to result in this particular landscape is mind-boggling.

Dear God

*First of all, thank you that you gave us the brains to reason,
and that you don't object when we question things, even your
existence. It must seem pretty ungrateful after all you've done
for me, and all the times I've felt your touch on my life.
How could I doubt after that? It's easy to say, 'Oh, if I saw a
miraculous healing I'd never doubt again', but thankfully
you've shown us the example of the disciples, who must have
seen incredible wonders but even they wavered.*

*But thank you that you show yourself to us again and again:
in big rocks and small grasses; in ways we can comprehend;
and in ways that are totally beyond our understanding.*

*And most of all you show yourself to us through the daily
care you have for us and our lives, for the little things we take
for granted, and for the big things we desperately need.*

Love, me.

The lazy hazy days of summer

On my list of least favourite things to do, cleaning comes pretty high, probably only surpassed by listening to double glazing salesmen. So why was I spending a beautiful Saturday afternoon cleaning the toilet? We weren't even expecting visitors. (It's the children's standard response when they see me cleaning; they ask, 'Is someone coming?') No, a busy week had meant that cleaning had to be put off (shame), and I just couldn't stand the state of the house any longer. So there I was, looking out at the sun and muttering under my breath. Doesn't dusting just drive you crazy? You smooth the cloth over the surface and watch as all the little particles of dead skin and detritus float around in the sun's rays, just waiting for you to turn your back, so they can settle down again. Oh I love it.

The children are just as bad. I spend half an hour sorting out the videos and tapes and putting them all back in the right boxes and on the right shelves only to find them spread all over the floor before I've even left the room! The problem with cleaning (what, another one?) is that it doesn't occupy your mind which is free to roam over things which, like the dust, are best left untouched.

Dear God

Now this is probably going to seem very unimportant and on the grand scale of things it is, but as it's something that occupies my time I feel I should have some say in it. So the question I want to ask you is, 'Why did you invent dust?'

See, I said it wasn't important.

I know it's my fault and if I was better organised I wouldn't have had to spend a sunny Saturday afternoon cleaning, but I'm not so I did. And it's not just dust, it's this whole cleaning thing – I can't seem to get the balance right. I really like the house when it's clean and shining but it's not often like that. I do make a special effort when people come round, but sometimes I put so much into cleaning and preparing food that by the time visitors arrive, I'm too tired to care and just wish they'd go. I love the idea of being a casual, laid-back, welcoming hostess but find it all such an effort that I end up with a monster headache, and fit for nothing except bed. I can't seem to get my priorities right. I'm definitely a Martha.

It's not as if I have posh friends who would expect everything to be perfect. I'm sure they would be happy with a Sainsbury's pizza eaten from third-best china. Well, I'm almost sure they would be but I'm also a bit afraid. Afraid that if I didn't make the effort, make it something worth coming for, they wouldn't come.

Please help me, God, to see friends as they are, not as people who have to be impressed, who have to be persuaded to like me. After all, nobody really chooses their friends on the strength of their cheesecake. Maybe I wish they did.

Lord, I need sorting out. Help.

Love, me.

Father . . . Father God

It was easy for Jesus. He was sure of his Father God's love. Not only that, but his earthly father, Joseph, who could easily have walked out on Mary, had, against the odds, stuck by Jesus and his mother. So it was easy for him to say, 'Father' and to teach his followers to say, 'Our Father'.

But what if it's not so easy for you? What if you've never known the love of an earthly father? What if your father image is one of rejection or abuse or disinterest?

It can be a big, maybe impossible, step then to trust someone who is called Father. How can you be sure that he won't let you down in the same way as your human father?

As good Christians we all know that whatever our problem we can take it to Jesus who because he became man and lived on this earth understands exactly how we feel. He's been there, done that, got the T-shirt. Well, maybe most things, but not this, we've already established that. Or have we?

'Why have you abandoned me?'

In spite of all his foreknowledge, certainty, closeness to his Father, that was Jesus' cry from the cross. When he needed him most, it appeared that his Father had let him down and it was no easier for Jesus to accept than it is for us.

Dear Father,

You don't know me but I'm your daughter. Ah yes, you remember now I see. You've always been aware of my existence but you've spent my lifetime ignoring it. You chose to abandon me without taking the trouble to get to know me. Was it something I said? No, it can't have been that, you weren't there to hear my first word, see my first smile, watch me find my feet. You missed a lot.

Do you have any regrets? Do you ever think of me or wonder what became of your child? Do you care about the damage you inflicted, damage that isn't completely repaired yet? But it's happening . . . slowly. The wounds and shame are being replaced by a sense of belonging, a sense of being loved and wanted by a father who is deserving of the name, valuable and of worth. Not an inconvenience to be discarded.

I have a lot to give, and I could have given to you much more than you will ever know.

Your daughter.

Dear 'Father'

That's not a word that lies easy on my lips. Far simpler to address you as Lord, creator, judge. 'Father' is getting too personal, too relational. Yet it's the way Jesus told us, commanded us, to address you. I know all the verses, the theology, the religious reasoning and I say 'great' but my heart's not convinced – I'm not there yet. There's still something missing. There are times when I feel as close to you as it is possible to be, and yes, I know faith isn't built on feelings anyway, but there is still that little gap between what I know and what I believe. Perhaps I'm looking for the complete answer, you know the sort of thing – get this sorted and I'll never doubt/be anxious/jealous, etc., again. Maybe I'm closer than I think.

I'm thankful that you choose to take on the role of father, that you want to set the standard: caring, devoted, interested, loving. I'm glad that my mother followed your example when it can't have been easy for her. I'm relieved that my conception wasn't a surprise to you, that you didn't say, 'well that was a silly mistake wasn't it?' I'm grateful that you stood by me as I struggled through school as a fatherless child. I'm glad that my life is going the way that you planned (with just a little side-tracking). I'm thankful for the example you've given me in the way my husband loves and treats our children.

I'm glad you're my Father.

Love, your child.

Tugging on the heartstrings

I've always been a sucker for those good old weepy songs, stories of lost loves. Songs like *Ebony Eyes* and *Tell Laura I Love Her*. Just thinking of them sends shivers down my spine. Actually I'm a sucker for anything that makes me cry: sentimental records, films with sad endings, films with happy endings. I was quite disappointed by *The English Patient*, it wasn't half as sad as I anticipated, I didn't even need my box of tissues. There's nothing I enjoy more than a film that makes me cry and there's one thing I'm sure of: my tear ducts are in perfect working order.

So why, when my cousin died of cancer, couldn't I shed a single tear? What was wrong with me?

Then one spring weekend a writing course, organised by the church, was held in a remote Welsh retreat. I went knowing what I wanted to write and given the topic, 'Echo', I made it fit. I don't usually write poetry but that's the way it came out.

Echo

The resonance of sound,
reverberating as it rebounds,
to return again and again
and again.
Each word reflected, mirrored,
echoing, echoing, echo.

Calling out to the heights,
your cry thrown back
at you,
a hollow shadow,
bereft of life.

And when your ears are ringing
and the mimicry
becomes too much
to bear,
what do you do?

When your questions
meet a resounding wall
of silence
and a jagged peace tears at your soul,
what do you do?

Turn off the tears,
shut down the heart,
build a wall to keep out pain
that buffets
and shakes
and threatens to undermine.

Let your heartstrings
be pulled
by sentimental songs,
reminding you of who you once were
and how you used to feel
before.
Before you became
an empty echo
of yourself.

Dear God

Break down the walls, help me feel again.

Love, me.

The lottery of life?

As I said, I've lost the ability to cry except over weepy songs or in self-pity. It wasn't always like that.

Crying is walking to the very edge of the sea when the tide's out and it's raining, and the salt from out there mingles with the salt from in here, and the wind carries the screams to the deep, and the dog sensing pain nuzzles but is soon bored and goes to find something more interesting.

Dear God

I used to know how to cry. I didn't save my tears for my own weaknesses. It isn't as if I've had a really bad life and I can't take any more. OK, the last few years have been a bit battering and I haven't understood you or why you've allowed things. She was so sure of you, to the moment she died she was convinced you would heal her. Her spirit was amazing, she wouldn't allow in the possibility that she might die, that would have been to doubt you after all, but how did you repay her faith? By letting her die. Her husband only has scorn for you now. Where there could have been miracles and rejoicing there was weeping.

And she's not the only one. How do you explain away your motives in letting a mother of four young children die? What excuses are we supposed to make?

'It's for the best.'

'God's in control, he knows what he's doing.'

Do you? Do you really, or is it just a lottery? Sorry your time's up.

The years are passing and I still can't follow your logic. Will I ever understand?

In the meantime, I'm hanging on, sometimes by my fingertips. Keep a tight hold, please.

Love, me.

The power of love

Cathy and Heathcliff. Ask just about anyone and they'll be able to tell you that these are characters in *Wuthering Heights*. Question them a bit more and, even if they're like me and have never read the book, they'll say it's the story of great love and passion.

I've never taken to these dark, sombre classics, and for someone who aspires to literary, if not wuthering, heights, that's quite a confession, so when *Wuthering Heights* was performed in our local theatre, it seemed an ideal opportunity to bring my education a step nearer completion. So with our mint humbugs tightly clutched in our hot little hands, we took our seats.

I know now why I never read it. Only one character was anything like pleasant, and as for Cathy, well, she needed a good shake, if not a slap.

But seriously, is it really the great love story it's made out to be? Can an emotion which is so destructive and harmful be called love?

I don't think so.

Dear God

If there's one thing I can be sure of it's that your love is never destructive. You'll never knock me down and leave me with no hope. That's not your style. You challenge, yes, but you don't humiliate and destroy.

I know when things are difficult or go wrong, I fall so easily into the trap of blaming myself, 'I deserve it because of the mess I am', and imagine that you're looking at me with disappointment on your face, that is if you can bring yourself to look at me at all. I revel in it, make a meal of it. I'm an expert in mental self-flagellation.

Self-esteem isn't a particular speciality of mine as you may have noticed. But I'm trying now, trying hard, to understand that you want to build up, that's your thing, strange as it may seem. You don't want to give up on me, you won't give up on me. You do look for repentance but when you're presented with an aching heart, you don't turn away and wait for more. Help me to grasp fully the nature of your love, to allow you in to repair the damage and strengthen the foundations.

Thank you that you communicate with us in all sorts of ways, when we least expect it. Keep me alert to your voice.

Love, me.

Patience is a virtue

Have you ever noticed when you go to the dentist, you seem to be in there for an hour at least? But when you come out and look at your watch, it turns out that it's only been five minutes? Perhaps it's just me. Or perhaps my dentist exists in a gap in the space/ time continuum. Who knows? Time is a strange thing.

Did you know that, in theory, time goes more slowly on the top of mountains and multi-storeys than it does at sea level? I suppose that means you take longer to grow old, which, considering the American obsession with ageing, might explain the number of skyscrapers in New York.

All this timely rumination came about after a walk around the cliffs one day. The Gower cliffs have a timeless quality about them, they're solid, secure, safe, unchanging.

Hang on a minute. These cliffs are old, millions of years old, and in their time they've seen plenty of upheaval. Some parts which started life as the sea bed are now standing to attention, almost vertical. Seeing that, you realise what a completely different time scale God works to.

Dear God

Teach me patience. It's not something I have in abundance.
I enjoy waiting for some things, like Christmas or my birthday.
Events where the anticipation is part of the excitement. But
for other things, like the resolution of problems or the times
promised which never seem to come, then it's harder to be
patient. I know exactly when my birthday will arrive so I can
wait with a certainty, but the answer to prayer, well, who
knows when that will be or what it will be?

It's for those times that I need to be able to trust you, to wait
patiently, to say that you know the outcome, and that you are
in control and that it will be for the best, even though I may not
think it. To tune into your view of time knowing you can see the
overall picture while I only see a nanosecond's-worth.

Next time I am impatient, take me back to those cliffs, help
me understand your time scale, help me realise how slowly
and carefully you put your plan for our world and my life into
operation.

You do have a sense of humour, Lord, don't you? Please give
me patience and give it to me NOW! (Sorry, I couldn't resist it.)

Love, me.

Boring

Some letters speak for themselves; this is one of those.

Dear God

*There are times when I think life would be so much easier if I
wasn't a Christian. Oh, most of the time, I appreciate you and
couldn't live without you, but every now and then these sneaky
thoughts creep in. Take now, for instance. If I wasn't a Christian
I wouldn't have to feel so guilty. Let's face it, the thing about
sin is that it's fun or makes you feel good, at least for a while.
You wouldn't want to do it otherwise. Having a good gossip or
moan about someone, bringing them down, lifts my spirits.
I know it shouldn't but it does, that's a fact.*

*Then of course, guilt arrives to weigh heavily on my shoulders.
Yes, I can say, 'sorry' but I know I don't really mean it and I'll do
it again. Well, there's a bit of me that means it and wishes I wasn't
so horrible, but there's also the bit which enjoys gossiping and
which tends to get the upper hand. Now I know you'll say, 'Well,
get it under control, say no', but it's not that easy. I've tried,
loads of times. Every time I say I won't do that again, whatever
it is, I pretty soon find myself falling down again, and again and
again. You must get bored of seeing me making a mess of my life
and listening to my whining cries of, 'Oh help me, God!' especially
as I'm not doing anything different; just the same old sins, over
and over again. I wouldn't blame you for switching off when I
come on. Even this letter is boring. Repetitive and boring.*

*Why do you put up with me, God?
I wouldn't.*

Love, me.

Daydream believer

If I were an actress, which I'm not, and was offered a role in my choice of soap opera, I know which one I'd choose. You can keep *Brookside, Corrie Street* or *Albert Square,* far too drab. *Neighbours* and *Home and Away* might have the sun and the sea but anyone joining the cast must realise the chances of them surviving much longer than the average chocolate eclair are not good. No, give me the healthy country air any time. It must be good for you, very few people pop their clogs in *The Archers.* You might be just a name on people's lips like Pru Forrest who hasn't been heard to speak for over twelve years but at least you know she's being well looked after in her twilight years in a pleasant little residential home where she gets regular visits from Uncle Tom. Anyway she will always live on through her marrow chutney.

What is it about soaps that attracts so many people? Otherwise sane, respectable members of the community, like me and my church elder, want, nay, *need* their daily fix of the everyday tale of country folk, or other less salubrious communities.

Is it escapism? A break from reality into a world where the sun might shine but I can rest secure in the knowledge that the characters will have more problems in one week than I'm likely to suffer in my lifetime. The trouble with escapism, however, is that the fantasy world can become more real than real life.

I'm a bit of a daydreamer. And of course in my dreams I'm always slimmer, more beautiful, more intelligent, more popular, more everything than in real life. And I can do anything. There are no barriers, the only thing that limits me is my imagination. Having an imagination is supposed to be an asset for an aspiring writer but sometimes it takes me over to a point where I almost don't want to come back. It's so much nicer in my pretend life. Real life becomes something to get through until I can escape again. I become remote, on a different plane, not much use to anyone because I'm too busy being wonderful.

I could get into the self-pity here and say, well wouldn't you if you were me? I'm hardly an inspiration to anyone. But something in me is changing.

Dear God

I think I'm finally getting to the place where I'm starting to believe that I am the person you created and I am the person you want me to be, strange as that seems. Lots of things have been happening recently which are bringing me to these conclusions. I'd like to say that it's you talking to me but those words don't sit easily. Some people speak of hearing from you as authoritatively as if they have the fax to confirm it, and maybe they are that sure, but you don't usually seem to talk to me like that. But I do believe that you're behind the messages that are gradually getting through my resistance, and I'm trying to listen.

Please keep speaking to me, however you choose (but make it clear, you know what I'm like, any excuse to feel sorry for myself!)

Love, me.

Wrinkles and all

Again if I were an actress, I'd probably be thinking about cosmetic surgery by now. On second thoughts, I'd have had it done years ago, before the effects of gravity became so obvious. Incidentally I love the way experts on antiques shows describe furniture as distressed – they should see what I see in the mirror if they want to talk about 'distressed'!

Anyway, back to the point, or not so much point as bulge. Bum and boobs are OK, they remain hidden except to my husband who seems inexplicably fond of them, which reminds me, I must tell him where I've hidden his glasses.

But the real tale-teller is my face. Little teacher's pet sneaking around exposing my secrets to all and sundry. It bears the scars of the ravages of time, which may sound poetic but we're definitely back in *Eastenders* territory.

The little wrinkles around my eyes, laughter lines, poetry again, I can cope with, it's the tractor furrows between my brows that cause me real grief. They've been there as long as I can remember. It's significant that the worry lines are the deepest – says a lot about my personality, I think.

I am envious of people who can say, 'What's the use of worrying?' and leave it at that. I know there's no use but it doesn't stop a worry becoming an obsession, which can take over my mind and disturb my peace.

And with a husband, three children and a dog, I've plenty of scope for concern.

Dear God

If there's one thing I would change about me, it wouldn't really be my furrowed brow; it would be the cause of the creases. You know, Lord, if there was an Olympic event of worrying, I'd take gold every time. And the thing is, I know it's pointless and I know Jesus said, 'Do not worry'. But that in itself isn't enough.

You understand, Lord, the way my body responds to anxiety, the real symptoms I experience. It's gone beyond a mental fretting. And you know how I've tried; I've physically hurled my anxieties onto you, as you told us. But it's as if I grab it back just as it's about to fly out of reach. I seize a corner, 'I'd better hang onto this, just in case'. Sometimes I feel guilty if I don't worry, because something might happen and I should worry.

Then my peace is destroyed.

This is a big one, Lord. It's not a little problem that will go away easily. It's inbuilt, part of me. I am totally dependent on you to act. I really need your Spirit in me to help me to let go of fear and anxiety. Continually, not just now and again. I want to be set free to be the person you want me to be but I'm held back. In the past, Lord, to my amazement, you have lifted burdens off me, taken them out of my reach – only after I've asked you, of course, you've never 'interfered'.

I need your Spirit now to help me throw away obsessive fear, and to help me keep saying 'no' when it tries to come back. You're the only one who can do this, Lord. I can't. On my own I'm defeated.

I don't expect problems to go away but they need to be in perspective. Help me put them there as they arise. Let me glimpse events from your perspective.

I need you.

'Turn your ear to me; when I call, answer me quickly.'

Love, me.

Fear of falling

I stood on the edge of the cliff today. Not for very long admittedly, but it was something.

You see, getting a book from the top shelf is a feat of daring for me, so standing peering over the edge of a cliff was an achievement. It's an irrational fear, this fear of, what is it? Heights? No, even I can see that simply being high can't hurt you, so it must be a fear of falling. Yet dissecting it calmly, from a distance, there's no logic to it. The Gower cliffs I stood on are solid and not prone to sudden rock slides; I wasn't so close to the edge as to be in danger of my foot slipping, and the odds against me having a sudden fainting spell at that precise moment and toppling off were enormous. So there's no real danger of falling.

But put me on the edge and my imagined fear produces real symptoms which stop me seeing the chicks in the nest below the crag, or the path down to the secret cove, or the way the waves wash over the mussel-covered rocks. You miss a lot by not going to the edge.

But I don't like getting too close to the edge. Which just about sums up my life.

Lord

When you came, you came to bring us life, life to the full,
and sometimes that means walking near the edge. Not taking
stupid risks, like jumping off and assuming you'll catch us, but
grabbing each minute and using it. I know that I'm a coward
with lots of fears, most of which are unjustified, but they stop
me going to the edge. They hold me back, my 'what-ifs'.

I don't want to be like that. I want to see all there is to see,
feel all there is to feel, soar to the heights. I can only do these
things if I'm confident that you're holding my hand. I know
you've held me in your hand but now I want to go that bit
further, just leaving my hand in yours, for safety, knowing
you won't let anything happen to me.

Take me to the edge, Father.

Count your blessings

1 A scrummy husband who loves me.

2 Three wonderful children.

3 Good health (in spite of my hypochondria!)

4 Enough money to eat well, be warm and enjoy some little extras.

5 A safe home.

6 Friends.

7 A soppy dog.

8 Living near the sea and the cliffs.

9 The gift of writing, and the opportunities it has afforded me over the last two years.

10 Being a child of God.

And so on, and so on, and so on . . . like seeing the first snowdrop of spring or eating an illicit custard slice (please excuse the crumbs).

Dear God,

Thank you with all my heart.

Love, me.

Exposed

You must have seen him. Tall, well-built, regular job. Green-haired, dirty, selling the *Big Issue*. Homeless. He's restless, his eyes can't quite stay with yours for long. That's if you give him the opportunity of course. And how many of us do? We're too wrapped up in our own lives to spare more than money for him. One pound to buy a warm glow. Cheap at the price.

My daughter, a budding journalist, wanted to interview a *Big Issue* vendor to find out what homelessness was really about. She arranged the interview and I dropped her off with strict instructions: don't go anywhere, just stay outside the shop, if he wants to show you where he sleeps, don't go. I don't know what I thought he would do. Who am I kidding? Of course I knew! Having done my shopping I returned to check the time she wanted to be collected only to find that she, and the vendor, had disappeared. My imagination ran riot. My daughter was dead, at best. Of course, she returned safely but not before my true feelings had come out of hiding.

Dear God

A hypocrite. That's what I see when I scrape the veneer off myself. A do-gooding hypocrite at that. One whose main aim in giving to charity is to experience a warm glow.

You don't let us get away with things like that though do you? You like to kick us in the shins and say, 'See the reality'. Well, I saw it today, the whole unpleasant truth.

Today, scenes Tarantino would have been proud of, ran through my mind just because my daughter had gone missing for half an hour. Well, that's forgivable, your daughter going missing like that. Anyone would do the same. Maybe, but would I have felt the same if she'd disappeared with a smartly dressed young executive? That's what really caught me short. Would my attitude have been different then? I think it would and that doesn't feel good. I saw dirty torn clothes and green hair, and visualised drink, drugs, and rape.

I deserved all my embarrassment on meeting him when he insisted on walking her back to the car (it's not safe for a young girl to walk through the bus station alone), and I needed the mirror held up to my soul.

Don't let me sit in judgement, God.

Yours, shamefaced.

Sunday

Some things beg the question, 'Did God have his mind on other things when he was making this?' Teeth, for example. Now there's nothing wrong with teeth in that they're very useful for making nice crunchy noises when you eat apples or whistling through if there's a big enough gap, but why did God design them with nerves? It's bad enough that I've got nerves; why do my teeth have to have them too?

Or why do things that are nice, like chocolate, have to be bad for you? Or make your teeth hurt?

On the other hand, I have to admit that God had some pretty good ideas. Golden retrievers, love, raspberries, the sun on the sea. One I really like is resting on the seventh day. (This isn't going to be a tirade against Sunday trading, I'm not that much of a hypocrite.) God got it right I reckon, so why do Christians make such hard work of it?

Sunday, the traditional day of rest which we kick up such a fuss to defend, is anything but restful for loads of people, including many churchgoers. Let's run through a typical Sunday in our house.

Having stayed up till the early hours in order to collect our daughter from a local nightclub, we are reluctant to get up, and remain under the bedclothes until the very last minute possible. Now that would be all right if it was only me to get ready for church, but it's two sons, plus daughter and friend as well. Getting party animals out of bed is not easy and sons demand porridge before they'll go anywhere. Meanwhile I hare around showering, dressing, intermittently nagging, 'Hurry up and eat your breakfast!', 'Have you washed?', 'You're not wearing that, are you?' and so on. Eventually I'm ready, the boys declare they've been ready for ages and there's no sign of the girls. Then the great shoe hunt commences. Take one dog, multiply him by ten shoes and you come up with the amount of time you waste searching for the missing ones. Finally they've all been located, but there's still no sign of the girls. 'We're going!' I scream up the stairs and make a big show of slamming the door behind me. They realise it's a bluff of course, because they take Sunday Club, and they know I'd be too embarrassed to turn up without them and let people down. So I get in the car, switch on the engine, turn the car around, and mutter under my breath, 'I've a good mind to go without them'. By the time they amble out, I'm revving like Damon Hill on the starting grid, and we screech off to arrive at church late. Just in time to hear the speaker say, 'Now let's put behind us everything that's been on our minds this week and concentrate on worshipping God'. I'm sorry but at that moment I'm in about as fit a state to concentrate on worshipping God as I am to join a nunnery.

The rest of the day's not much better, routinely planned out to ensure we can squeeze in everything we have to do. Where does it say in the Bible that we should have meetings on our day of rest? Or where does it say that you have to have a good excuse not to go at least once? And yet how many of us still feel guilty? Or is it just me?

Dear God

I'm grumbling again. I don't mean to, it's just that I'm tired. No, I'm not tired, I'm worn out. Worn out by nagging. Why is it, Lord, that the children, the minute they reach church, change from the non-communicating, got-out-of-bed-the-wrong-side little monsters that sulked in the car with me, into happy, pleased-to-see-their-mates Persil-white darlings? Why am I left a wreck, fit for nothing, least of all praise and thankfulness? This can't be what you intended when your family started meeting together. Although, come to think of it, family gatherings can be quite fraught affairs. But that's not the way it should be for Christians surely?

It's not as if we belong to some really strict church. Ours is very laid-back, yet looking around in the mornings, there are parents everywhere who, if they're not looking stressed at the start, soon change after trying to keep little Tracy amused for three-quarters of an hour or so.

It's good being part of a family but do we have to get together, all together, quite so often? Would you mind if we didn't? If instead of going to the Sunday morning meeting we just spent the time in our own families or with close friends. If we tried finding out about each other and caring for each other. Mind you, there are members of the family I'm not bothered if I don't see regularly (that's putting it politely). Is that dreadful? There's a limit to how much caring and sharing a mere mortal, especially one like me, can do.

I'm not saying that we shouldn't ever meet but somehow the way the first Christians did it seems more relaxed, more natural.

Perhaps I've lost my way. If you're the centre of the church, then our focus should be on you, and you're the reason we're there, but not necessarily on a Sunday morning. I'd much rather praise you when I'm where I can touch you, where I can smell you or feel you. When praise is instinctive; when all I can do is say thank you. Or when life is so bad, when there's so much doubt, and fear, that all I can do is fall on you and trust you, and thank you for not letting go.

Help me to live a life of worship, Lord, where each move I make is praise to you. From where I'm sitting that seems like an impossibility but they say nothing's impossible for you. Hope they (whoever they might be) are right.

Love from, the edge (but I'm hanging on).

I'll be there for you
(unless something more interesting comes along)

'Who's the cake for, Mum?' a sorrowful little voice asks. I look around; it's not a pretty sight. My son is drooling pathetically and can't believe his ears when I say it's for us. I very rarely make cakes these days – they only get eaten. I mean they get eaten too quickly! Cakes are devoured faster than I can make them so it's quicker and cheaper to buy some at Kwik-Save (who thus live up to their name).

The children have the same sort of attitude to me cleaning. 'Is someone coming?' they say. Honestly, anyone would think I never did any cleaning. Although I have to admit I do make a special effort to spruce the place up (and it's not easy with a hairy dog, three untidy children, and an equally untidy mum in the house) when we have visitors. Like last weekend. Or so we expected.

The previous Sunday father-in-law had suggested that they might come down to stay the coming weekend, so I rushed around like a maniac. I wasn't going to be shown up for the slut I am. Anyway, that was the last we heard of that idea; they didn't come and all my cleaning went to waste. That's the thing about cleaning, the effects last an even shorter time than cake. What lasts a whole lot longer is my grumbling.

I suppose all of us in our dealings with others expect certain things; exactly what they are depends on the closeness and type of our relationship. Inevitably there will be times when we are disappointed. Sometimes it won't matter; sometimes it matters a lot; and sometimes the resulting resentment can worm its way in so deeply that its poison spreads and colours everything we are.

Is it our fault for expecting too much? When a dear and trusted Christian friend said, 'Don't expect anything of anyone, then you won't be disappointed', I was horrified, it seemed such a hopeless statement. And I kept on expecting.

When I was little I was part of an old-fashioned extended family. Of course there were rows, the aunties fell out, called each other names, but at the first sign of a problem or crisis, they were there for each other. They put aside their differences, their own needs, and corporately supported each other. I grew up thinking that was normal. Perhaps it was only normal for me, Nowadays finding someone who's not going to let you down seems a lot harder (if only life were like *Friends*). Sometimes it even seems that God has let me down, but that's another letter.

Dear God

I think it goes back a long time, not that that's any excuse. Old resentments rearing their heads. Things I'd hoped I'd forgiven, easier than forgetting. The letting down, not living up to expectations. Perhaps it was my fault, making assumptions.

Then dealing with it. It's said, 'You don't have to feel it if your intention is good, God will sort it out', and, 'You can forgive someone instantly, rebuilding trust takes time'. In other words, you can say the phrase and want to mean it even if you don't feel it, and if you keep battling and refusing to wallow in hurt, then it'll be all right in the end. But it's not as easy as that, Lord.

If trust gets chipped at, the backward step is much greater in proportion, isn't it? It's like a sand dune; for each three forward steps, you go back two. A big sandslide and it's even possible to end up where you started, wallowing in recriminations.

Is it all my fault? I know I'm too quick to criticise, dislike. To find problems where there are none. I'm certainly not a good advert for Christianity. I let you down, Lord, I hold things inside, things which happened long ago, which I find so hard to really let go of. Lord, you know how many times I've tried; I've said it and physically thrown the hurts away. And for a while it feels better but then something happens and before I know where I am I'm dredging them up again.

I start off with good intentions (on the road to hell) but they just choke me, and I find myself reluctant to even try to mend fences. I need you so much in this, Father. I cannot do this on my own. I'm crying out to you. I need a fresh start, I need the will to forgive, I need the power to forget. Only you can give me those things. I'm not a very nice person. I'd relish the opportunity to tell people of my grievances, but only those I could rely on for sympathy, of course. See what I mean – not very nice at all.

Looking for someone else to blame won't help, it won't take away my guilt, only you can do that. Only you can change me. Only you can make me want to change.

Help me in this, Lord. It's screwing up a part of my life. Knowing there is a big chunk of me you wouldn't be happy with makes me incomplete, unable to function properly.

For all our sakes, help me, Lord.

Love, me

The test

Just before Anna's seventeenth birthday a new member of the family arrived. Her name's Daisy, she's very beautiful, and she's a white Volkswagen Beetle. Dad had finally been worn down and had given in to the pleading to swap the trusty old family Montego for this, this angel of delight. Anna already had the shades, the hippie gear, now she had the transport; the only thing left was to learn to drive it.

Anna has never failed anything in her life. She took it for granted that the driving test would be another notch on her belt. I wasn't so sure.

The trouble was that at the time, her life seemed to be falling apart at the seams.

Dear God

Anna has her driving test today. I don't know what to pray. I'll leave it up to you.

If she's ready to be on the road alone, then please help her to pass.

If she's not, then it's better if she fails. Whatever, please help her to stay calm and do her best. Thank you.

Love, me.

Dear God

When I said it was up to you, and if she wasn't ready I didn't want her to pass, I didn't mean that she should fail quite so spectacularly.

Was it really necessary, God? Did she have to come home quite so demoralised? Just one or two minor things would have been enough. As it is she's lost all her confidence and is reluctant to get back in the car.

What do you mean 'You should be happy then'? I admit I was nervous with her driving but I'm like that with most people these days. It would come in useful if she was able to drive and it would be another hurdle out of the way. It's not just that we've spent a lot of money on her lessons, it's more than that.

For years she's been waiting for the day she passes her test. She assumed it would happen easily. She's never failed anything in her life; and now she has, she doesn't know how to cope with it. Was it meant to be a lesson in dealing with failure, picking yourself up and getting on with it? Preparing her for life in the real world? If that was the case, the timing was rubbish. When you're only just managing to struggle up a sand dune the last thing you want is to be knocked down to the bottom again.

Not that I'm much use; I don't encourage her to come out in the car and practise. I suppose we both need encouragement.

Over to you.

Love, me.

Wedded bliss

'Welcome to Blackpool Pleasure Beach! Ride the Big One, visit the side-shows . . . oh, and why not take the opportunity to get married before you leave?' This is for real, this is now, not some futuristic nightmare. Today it is possible to get spliced, tie the knot, get hitched, amidst the glittery tat, the thrills and spills of the country's foremost leisure park, which is just one of any number of unusual places that have been licensed for weddings.

Hotels, of course, have quickly cashed in by offering a full service starting with the ceremony and ending with overnight accommodation for guests. And why not? With the numbers of people professing little or no faith rising all the time, it's certainly less hypocritical to have a civil ceremony, and it's not the venue or even the form of service that worries me. What does concern me is the attitude of those getting married.

Many young couples seem to be starting their married life not expecting it to last forever, and if, even on your wedding day, you don't have that hope and expectation, the future doesn't seem too bright.

My children are all a long way off marrying (I hope) but I'm a normal mum, and I do dream of seeing them with wonderful white weddings, in a joyful and meaningful church service.

Dear God

I know it's a bit early to start worrying about these things and I've got plenty of time, but when I look around me I can't help but see things which don't feel right. Marriages for convenience or habit or just because it's simpler; marriages which have very little chance of lasting beyond the feel-good stage. And I don't want that for my children, Lord.

I want to see them married, Lord; I want to see them settled in a strong relationship, I want to know they'll have their partner to stand by them, and I want it to be for ever. Is that asking too much? Oh, yes, and I would like them to marry Christians.

Adam and Eve, man and woman, husband and wife, it was all your idea, so I don't think I'm asking for things outside the norm. I'm very thankful for my own marriage. Of course, it hasn't been problem free, we've done 'in sickness or in health', 'for better or for worse', and thankfully we've only had 'richer'. Through it all knowing that you're there is the comfort, Lord, the strength - it's not mine. In so many situations, I find myself thinking, 'How do non-Christians manage without God to rely on?' I might be accused of using you as a crutch, and I suppose that's true in a way, but it's not just a broken leg that needs supporting, it's a recovering life you support, underpinning everything that I do.

Be that firm foundation for my children, God. Help them to grow in their relationship with you and to find the right partners, with whom they'll be able to face the future, expecting that future to be together. I know that Christian marriages aren't immune from problems and divorce still happens, but with you involved, there is still some hope and expectation. Give them great expectations, Lord.

Love, me.

Puppy power

A book that deals with my life, its pain and pleasures, wouldn't be complete without mention of the family pets. We're currently the devoted subjects of Harvey, our golden retriever, a lolloping, slobbering, crotch-nosing, distant relative of the yeti, who likes to think that life revolves around him, and who am I to argue?

Then there's Fred, Barney and Bam-Bam, the goldfish. They are inveterate liars. As soon as I appear in the room they rush to the side of the tank and mouth pathetically, trying to convince me they haven't been fed. And very persuasive they are too.

In the last few years we've also had a cat and more recently, a hamster. The cat came with the house, and let us down shamefully when he ate a gerbil we were looking after for a friend. The hamster belonged to twelve-year-old Neil, although his initial enthusiasm waned when the only signs we had that Nibbles was alive were the ghostly midnight squeaking of her wheel, and the ever-decreasing level of food in her dish. In fact, it was the piled-high dish of food that alerted us, one sad day, to the fact that Nibbles was no more. It's strange how attached you can get to pets, even furry rodents who do nothing.

Shortly after we had discovered Nibbles' still little body, I found Neil lying on the sofa, cuddling a cushion. 'How long will I feel like this?' he cried. 'I'm never going to have another pet, I can't stand this.' And this was all of thirty minutes suffering he had gone through.

By late afternoon he was planning what to get next, 'but not just yet'.

It's said that grieving over pets helps children to learn about death and prepares them for the loss of loved ones of the human kind. But it still hurts and standing by knowing there's nothing you can say or do to wipe out the pain is hard.

Dear God

Were pets your idea, I wonder? Or did animals have a purely
functional role in the garden of Eden? Whatever, I think they're
an excellent invention. Harvey is sitting beside me now as I
write this. He's just come in and he looks half-asleep, as if he's
not sure what he's doing here. He's smelly and he's muddy and
I love him. Perhaps that should teach me a lesson about you!

I'm really grateful for his companionship and love, for his
gentle nature and the protection he offers all of us, but
especially the children, seeming instinctively to understand
their vulnerability.

I'm glad, most of the time anyway, of the opportunity to
get out and walk with him, for the exercise, the fresh air, the
chance to think, and to appreciate your creation.

Lord, I don't want to try and find any clever messages in
pets, that's not what this prayer is about. It's just a simple
thank you for the good things and the strength to cope with
the bad.

Love, me.

Zzzzzzz

I'm usually ready for bed by about ten o'clock, which makes the prospect of getting through the rest of the day rather daunting. Tiredness is an occupational hazard, it comes with the job of parenthood. My husband claims it started for him with my first labour: I spent the night in bed dozing while he had to sit on a hard chair next to me (apparently the nurses told him to go home, it would be a long time yet, but I insisted on him being there, he says, and he hasn't let me forget it.) Years of disturbed sleep were to follow that first experience. If it wasn't babies crying, it was babies vomiting, or babies being ill. Within a couple of years your sleep pattern is so disturbed, you can't sleep normally even if you have the opportunity.

I suppose there was a short period when our nights weren't too bad. There must have been, I just can't remember it. It didn't last long. Now we're into the late night disco-ing. Anna's evenings don't start until 10.30 and go on well into the night. Even if she's with a group of friends and is getting a taxi home, it's not possible to sleep properly until she's in.

And sleeping late in the mornings isn't an option either. We're woken either by the dog who needs to go out or Robert preparing for his paper round. Speaking of the dog reminds me that sleep can be ruled out on nights when there is a full moon: he will get us up repeatedly so he can go and sit and stare at it. We have to pray for a cloudy sky on such nights.

Still I suppose I do have old age to look forward to. They say old people need less sleep. I will be able to get out videos of all those films that I started watching in the eighties and nineties, and find out what happened at the end. That is if I can stay awake.

Dear God

*Human beings must be pretty resilient, being able to survive
on so little sleep. I thank you for the strength you've given me,
and the freedom from illness. I might grumble but I wouldn't
have missed it for the world. Our children are so precious to us,
we would do anything for them. Including staying up late and
ferrying them about. I wonder if we've been too protective –
can you be too protective? We seem to fuss more than other
parents. Please help our children to understand that we do it
because we love them. And please help us to let go, to see when
it's time to let them find their own feet, knowing we've done all
we can to ensure their feet are on the ground.*

*It's such a delicate balance, Lord. Help us to get close to
being right. We can only do our best, what we think is best.
It's all new to us too, we don't have diplomas in parenthood.
(Would I pass?) Help us not to rush into decisions, to think
before we speak, to trust them.*

*I value all of the experiences of parenthood even though
sometimes I may wish I hadn't experienced some of them. Now,
Lord, give strength to the weary, take me soaring with you.*

Love, me.

True love

We disagree about most things. For a start I'm a Christian and he's not. He leans to the right; I have leftish tendencies. I can be moved to tears by something I see; he says it's their own fault. He's English; I'm Welsh. I love reading; he hates books. He loves a glass of malt whiskey; I have to go to the other side of the room because I can't bear the smell. He's bossy; I'm put upon. He's organised; I'm untidy. I'm easily distracted; he's single-minded. He likes *Terminator*; I like *Sense and Sensibility*. He cleans his shoes; I can't remember what colour mine are.

And yet we love each other. I love the way that when we're watching the news and the reporter says something happened at Prestatyn, he'll say, 'Press what in?' I love the way we both associate the same songs with events or things that happened. And sometimes I'll say something knowing what his response will be, and if he doesn't say it straightaway I look at him enquiringly, and he'll realise what I'm waiting for and he'll say it. I love it when we both say we're dieting and then we devour a large bar of chocolate watching a video. I love it when he has a busy day at work and I phone him and say, 'Meet me for lunch?' and he says, 'OK'.

I love someone who's bossy and grumpy and he loves someone who's disorganised and selfish. Love is strange.

True love is about knowing someone really well. It's about knowing his little habits and loving him for them. It's about knowing his faults and loving him in spite of them. True love can be expressed in a word, a touch, a look, a kiss . . . or death on a cross.

Dear God

*Love is blind. How else can you explain the way people love
each other and put up with each other? No, it can't be blind,
it has its eyes opened and still loves. It's very odd the way we
love each other; sometimes he drives me mad; sometimes, no
doubt, I drive him mad, but we manage to cling on to something
bigger than minor irritations.*

*It's the same with the children, I suppose, only more so.
They, too, can drive me mad, but I love them. If I can see all
this love and, in spite of my human failings, can express it and
feel it, and know that I could never not love them, why do I
struggle with your love for me? Why do I find your love so hard
to believe in? Why do I imagine that every little, or not so little,
misdemeanour, is another black mark which will make me less
lovable? Do I love my children any less when they've been
naughty? Of course not.*

*Do you really love me because of my good points? And in
spite of my bad habits? Do you really love me just because I'm
me, your creation, your child?*

*I know you love me but there's a big difference between
knowing and grasping the truth of that love. Maybe it's just
warm feelings that I'm looking for. My faith isn't built on feelings,
it has stronger foundations than that so I can continue believing
even if I don't feel . . . even if I don't feel.*

But a cuddle now and then would help.

Love, me.